Castles

LEVEL 11

DECODABLES BY jump!

Teaching Tips

Lime Level 11

This book focuses on developing reading independence, fluency, and comprehension.

Before Reading

- Ask readers what they think the book will be about based on the title. Have them support their answer.

Read the Book

- Encourage readers to read silently on their own.
- As readers encounter unfamiliar words, ask them to look for context clues to see if they can figure out what the words mean. Encourage them to locate boldfaced words in the glossary and ask questions to clarify the meaning of new vocabulary.
- Allow readers time to absorb the text and think about each chapter.
- Ask readers to write down any questions they have about the book's content.

After Reading

- Ask readers to summarize the book.
- Encourage them to point out anything they did not understand and ask questions.
- Ask readers to review the questions on page 23. Have them go back through the book to find answers. Have them write their answers on a separate sheet of paper.

This edition is published by arrangement with Booklife Publishing.

North American adaptations © 2024 Jump!
5357 Penn Avenue South
Minneapolis, MN 55419
www.jumplibrary.com

Decodables by Jump! are published by Jump! Library.

Library of Congress Cataloging-in-Publication Data is available at www.loc.gov or upon request from the publisher.

ISBN: 979-8-88996-942-6 (hardcover)
ISBN: 979-8-88996-943-3 (paperback)
ISBN: 979-8-88996-944-0 (ebook)

Photo Credits

Images are courtesy of Shutterstock.com. With thanks to Getty Images, Thinkstock Photo and iStockphoto. Cover - Marti Bug Catcher. 4–5 – Keattikorn, Miguel Almeida, sPhillip Minnis. 6–7 – IR Stone, Tomas Marek. 8–9 – Jelena Aloskina, StepStock, Jopics. 10–11 – Anneka, Nejron Photo. 12–13 – Everett Collection, Franck Boston. 14–15 – Esteban De Armas. 16–17 – Matt Gibson, Wozzie. 18–19 – pzAxe, Kristyna Mladkova. 20–21 – canadastock, Adrian Stanica.

Table of Contents

What Are Castles?

Castles are buildings that were made for very important people. They were homes built for **defense**. Castles are found all over the world, from China to the United Kingdom. For hundreds of years, castles were homes, meeting places, and defenses. They had many uses. Kings and queens often built castles to show how important they were.

The people who lived in castles were very rich and important, so castles had to protect the people inside. A fortress is a building used for defense. It is different from a castle because no one lives in it. A palace, on the other hand, is a home for important people. But it does not have defenses.

Fortress

Palace

Types of Castles

A thousand years ago, most castles were motte and bailey castles. These castles had two parts. The wooden keep was built on a mound of earth called a motte. Being high above ground made it easier to see attackers coming. The homes were built lower down on the ground. They were surrounded by a wall. This was called the bailey.

Motte and bailey castles were made of wood. Then, people started building stone keep castles. These were similar to motte and bailey castles, but they were made of stone. They were much stronger than wooden castles. Next, people made concentric castles. Concentric castles were stone castles with at least two walls around the bailey.

Stone keep castle

Concentric castle

Life in a Castle

Castles may have been used for defense, but they were also homes. Many people lived and worked in a castle. The people who owned castles were very rich. They were often royals, such as kings or queens, or nobles known as lords or ladies. These people lived in the nicest rooms in the castle.

Soldiers also lived in castles. A soldier's job was to defend the castle and protect the people who lived there. Servants also lived in castles. Servants had many different jobs, such as washing clothes and even emptying out the toilets! Many castles had a jester. The jester performed shows for the rich people to watch.

Soldier

Servant

Jester

Food and Drink

The kitchen was one of the busiest rooms in the castle. In the kitchen, cooks made food for everyone in the castle. Sometimes they might have had to feed hundreds of people in one day! In the Middle Ages, people ate very different food than what we eat today. Sometimes, they even ate swans.

They did not use plates. Instead, they used flat pieces of stale bread as plates. This bread was then given to poor people or animals to eat. While poor people were eating stale bread, rich people went to **banquets** and ate the best meats, cheeses, and fruits.

Attacking Castles

The people who owned castles were very rich. Everyone knew that if someone owned a castle, it would be full of their money and treasure! However, there were other reasons to attack castles. The people who owned castles usually ruled the land around it. A castle might be attacked by people who want to take that land.

When castles were built of wood, the easiest way to attack was with fire. Stone castles, however, do not burn easily. To get into a stone castle, people had to break through the walls using pickaxes. If the walls were too thick to break through, they would dig underneath the walls.

Siege!

A siege was a way of taking control of an enemy's castle. In a siege, an army would surround a castle, and no one would be allowed in or out of the castle. The attacking army would wait. Sometimes they waited weeks or even months.

Eventually, the people inside the castle would get so hungry that they had to **surrender**. However, the people inside the castle would do everything they could to avoid this. During a siege, people sometimes had to eat horses and even rats! Meanwhile, the people outside the castle continued to attack. They even built special siege weapons.

Defending Castles

The people who built castles knew that people would try to attack them, so castles were made for defense. Most castles were built in places that were hard to reach. Some were built by rivers, the sea, or special ditches called **moats**. They were often built high up on hills so the people inside could see enemies coming.

Castle windows were very small. They were wide enough for someone inside the castle to shoot an arrow through but small enough that it would be very difficult to get an arrow through from outside.

Thin windows are known as arrow slits.

No More Castles

Over time, people built bigger and more powerful weapons. Eventually, **gunpowder** and cannons were invented. Cannons shoot large, heavy metal balls at very high speeds. These weapons were so strong they could break through even the strongest castle walls. These inventions changed the world and meant that castles were no longer a good defense.

The castles left standing were either **abandoned** or changed into fancy homes. Instead of being used as defense, people only used castles to show everyone how much money they had. Many castles were left to fall apart. These are called ruins. Many castles are still standing. Some castles can still be visited!

Castles Around the World

There are many castles all over the world. There are thousands of castles in England that are still standing, such as Alnwick Castle and Dover Castle. Germany has more castles than any other country in the world. Neuschwanstein Castle in Germany is thought to have inspired many famous stories and films.

Neuschwanstein Castle

Many other castles have also inspired famous stories. For example, author Bram Stoker used pictures of Bran Castle to come up with the castle of his most famous creation: Count Dracula. So, while castles may have been built as defenses, they now have many uses, such as inspiring stories and teaching us about the past.

Bran Castle

Index

How to Use an Index

An index helps us find information in a book. Each word has a set of page numbers. These page numbers are where you can find information about that word.

Page numbers

Example: balloons 5, 8–10, 19

Important word

This means page 8, page 10, and all the pages in between. Here, it means pages 8, 9, and 10.

Questions

1. What were the first castles made out of?

2. In the Middle Ages, what did people use instead of plates?

3. Why did people stop building castles?

4. Using the Table of Contents, can you find which page you can read about life in a castle?

5. Using the Index, can you find a page in the book about soldiers?

6. Using the Glossary, can you define what banquets are?

Glossary

abandoned:
Left behind.

banquets:
Formal meals for large groups of people.

defense:
The ability to protect from harm or attack.

gunpowder:
A powder that can easily explode and is used in some weapons, such as bullets and cannons.

moats:
Ditches that are wide and deep, filled with water, and dug around castles.

surrender:
To give up.